Relationship Skills in the Bible

Scriptural Principles of Relating to Others

Bisi Oladipupo

Springs of life publishing

Contents

Dedication

To Jesus Christ, my Lord and Saviour—to Him alone that laid down His life that I might have life eternal. To Him that led captivity captive and gave gifts unto men (Ephesians 4:8). One of those gifts is writing!

Foreword

If you have been alive for any length of time, you will agree that relating with people well is a skill we all have to learn. Knowing how to relate to people is necessary if you intend to walk in love and live in peace.

The Bible says, "*If any of you lack wisdom, let him ask of God, that giveth to all men liberally, and upbraideth not; and it shall be given him*" (James 1:5). Therefore, we can always ask for wisdom when relating to others.

As the scriptures are full of many relationships, we can learn some relationship principles from Scripture. This is what this book aims to do.

At the end, my prayer is that you will be skilful enough to foster healthy relationships, know when to let go of people, and above all, stay and walk in love, which is a commandment for every believer.

I also hope that you will be able to discern when to hold onto relationships and make an effort to invest in them.

Bisi Oladipupo

Chapter One

There is a Friend That Sticks Closer Than a Brother

S ome people have an upper privilege in that they have come from large families. Some people have many blood brothers and sisters from the same parents.

In such cases, it is easy to develop good and meaningful lifelong relationships. In other words, you should have one flourishing relationship amid diverse interactions. However, this is not the case with everyone. If you happen to come from a small family, or for some reason, your immediate family is not around, do not despair. The Lord can give you a friend that is even closer than a brother.

"A man that hath friends must shew himself friendly: and there is a friend that sticketh closer than a brother" (Proverbs 18:24).

From the above scripture, firstly, if we want friends, we must be friendly. If we are not friendly, it's very simple. The opposite will apply.

A good example of a friend that was closer than a brother in Scripture was the relationship between David and Jonathan. The Scripture says, *"Then Jonathan and David made a covenant, because he loved him as his own soul"* (1 Samuel 18:20).

We know that this relationship was God-ordained because Jonathan was able to help David and protect him when Saul, his own father, wanted to kill David. Our God is all-knowing. Could this be why Jonathan and David became very good friends? What lesson can we learn from this?

There might be times that some friends are even closer than family members. Embrace them; be friendly as you have no idea why they are in your life.

Chapter Two

Invest in others

We need to learn to invest in others. This is part of seeking first the kingdom of God and His righteousness (Matthew 6:33). God loves people, and so should we.

Now, let us look at an excellent example of someone who invested in another person and reaped great results. Mordecai and Esther. If Mordecai did not invest in Esther when she was young and took her as his own daughter (Esther 2:7), all that happened would not have occured. Mordecai had access to Esther because he had been there for her from a young age. He was then able to reveal to Esther the plans of destroying the Jews. You can read the full account in the Book of Esther.

Sometimes, the Lord will also bring "work in process" people into our lives. Yes, we are all "work in process", but sometimes, your whole assignment, which might be for a season, is to help another person grow up.

Here, Paul is speaking:

I beseech thee for my son Onesimus, whom I have begotten in my bonds: Which in time past was to thee unprofitable, but now profitable to thee and to me (Philemon 1:10-11).

We can see from this scripture that Paul had made some investment in Onesimus' life. We need discernment to know who to invest in, as such people might be pillars in society and God's kingdom tomorrow. Everyone is important to the agenda of God's Kingdom, and sometimes, you might be the mentor that the Lord will use to bring out the best in others.

Chapter Three

Know when to withdraw your foot

A well-known minister of the gospel that l listen to says "people have choking points", which l believe is true.

When we relate to others, we should discern how much space a person has given us in their lives and adjust accordingly. For example, you might be able to call Ms R, a friend, at 11 pm, and it's okay, but if you call someone else at that time, you might create a problem. The same applies to how many times you visit a person. Each relationship is different, and we need discernment.

"Hast thou found honey? eat so much as is sufficient for thee, lest thou be filled therewith, and vomit it. Withdraw thy foot from thy neighbour's house; lest he be weary of thee, and so hate thee" (Proverbs 25:16-17).

The above scripture is self-explanatory. We need to know other people's choking points. In other words, when your presence is getting too much for them.

Chapter Four

Don't impose yourself on others

The Lord does not impose Himself on us. This is why only those that seek will find (Matthew 7:7).

The Lord asked Peter to follow Him; he left all and followed the Lord (Matthew 4:18-20). However, when Jesus Christ asked the rich man to sell his goods and follow Him, the rich man declined (Matthew 19:16-23).

What was Jesus' response? Jesus respected the rich man's decision and left him.

"Behold, I stand at the door, and knock: if any man hear my voice, and open the door, I will come in to him, and will sup with him, and he with me" (Revelation 3:20).

The Lord does not impose Himself on people. Instead, the Lord knocks and gives people an opportunity or choice to respond.

In our relationships, we must not impose ourselves on others.

Not everyone will want to be your friend, and that is fine. We must walk, stay in love, and then apply wisdom when relating to others.

Chapter Five

Not everyone will like you

There will always be people that don't like you. For example, during Jesus Christ's earthly ministry, some disciples left Him after a while.

Why did they turn back? Because they misunderstood what Jesus Christ, our Lord, was saying. In my opinion, those disciples lacked discernment.

"For my flesh is meat indeed, and my blood is drink indeed. He that eateth my flesh, and drinketh my blood, dwelleth in me, and I in him. As the living Father hath sent me, and I live by the Father: so he that eateth me, even he shall live by me. This is that bread which came down from heaven: not as your fathers did eat manna, and are dead: he that eateth of this bread shall live for ever. These things said he in the synagogue, as he taught in Capernaum. Many therefore of his disciples, when they had heard this, said, This is an hard saying; who can hear it"? (John 6:55-60).

It is the spirit that quickeneth; the flesh profiteth nothing: the words that I speak unto you, they are spirit, and they are life. But there are some of you that believe not. For Jesus knew from the beginning who they were that believed not, and who should betray him. And he said, Therefore said I unto you, that no man can come unto me, except it were given unto him of my Father. **From that time many of his disciples went back, and walked no more with him** (John 6:63-66).

We can see Jesus Christ, our Lord's perspective, about the matter: *"But there are some of you that believe not. For Jesus knew from the beginning who they were that believed not, and who should betray him"* (John 6:64).

Therefore, some of the disciples that followed Jesus Christ, our Lord before, believed not, and that was why they turned back. It was not what Jesus Christ said. What Jesus Christ said just triggered and exposed what was already in their hearts.

We need to pray that the Lord gives us discernment when relating to people. This is why some people will suddenly throw surprises at you. Jesus Christ, our Lord, knew already from the beginning and allowed them to follow Him. What a gracious Lord! We can assume that they had an opportunity to judge themselves. Jesus Christ allowed them to follow Him until they decided to leave.

Have you ever said anything innocently, and someone took offence into the meaning of it? This is what happened to Jesus Christ. Their hearts were exposed, and instead of judging themselves or believing the best, they turned back.

Jesus Christ knew who He was, and He was secure in the Father's love. Likewise, we must be secured in the love of God. We must walk in love and keep our hearts right at all times.

The Bible also tells us that they hated Jesus Christ without a cause.

"But this cometh to pass, that the word might be fulfilled that is written in their law, They hated me without a cause" (John 15:25).

"Let not them that are mine enemies wrongfully rejoice over me: neither let them wink with the eye that hate me without a cause" (Psalms 35:19).

Don't take it personally when people don't like you. It happened to Jesus without a cause.

Chapter Six

Open rebuke is necessary sometimes

Sometimes, it is necessary to rebuke a person openly in the presence of others.

Them that sin rebuke before all, that others also may fear (1 Timothy 5:20).

When Peter yielded to his flesh and the enemy, Jesus Christ, our Lord, rebuked Peter openly (Matthew 16:23).

If you look at the content of the verse, the other disciples were there.

20 Then charged he his disciples that they should tell no man that he was Jesus the Christ. 21 From that time forth began Jesus to shew unto his disciples, how that he must go unto Jerusalem, and suffer many things of the elders and chief priests and scribes, and be killed, and be raised again the third day. [22] Then Peter took him, and began to rebuke him, saying, Be it far from thee, Lord: this shall not be unto thee. [23] But he turned, and said unto Peter, Get thee behind me, Satan: thou art an offence unto me: for thou savourest not the things that be of God, but those that be of men. [24] Then said Jesus unto his disciples, If any man will come after me, let him deny himself, and take up his cross, and follow me (Matthew 16:20-24).

In both verses twenty and twenty-four, we can see Jesus addressing His disciples. Therefore, the rebuke was in the presence of His disciples.

What did Peter do? We have no account that Peter took offence. On the contrary, he took it well and learned from it. We know that we can't find a similar account of this in the Bible again. Peter later became a great Apostle and mighty man of God. Therefore, we know that Peter took the rebuke well and repented.

This is what we have to do when we are told off, even if it happens in public. We must remember that the Lord chastises whom He loves.

For whom the Lord loveth he correcteth; even as a father the son in whom he delighteth (Proverbs 3:12).

For whom the Lord loveth he chasteneth, and scourgeth every son whom he receiveth (Hebrews 12:6).

Has someone told you off? Then don't abort the relationship because of that; just amend and do what is necessary to make the corrections.

We should also allow those that are wiser or more experienced in our lives to correct us when necessary and let us take the correction well.

It is part of growing up and necessary for some types of relationships.

Chapter Seven

Sometimes, it is best to mind your own business

Have you ever wondered why some people get involved with something that has nothing to do with them?

"He that passeth by, and meddleth with strife belonging not to him, is like one that taketh a dog by the ears." (Proverbs 26:17)

"Interfering in someone else's argument   is as foolish as yanking a dog's ears." (Proverbs 26:17; NLT)

"Like one who grabs a dog by the ears [and is likely to be bitten]Is he who, passing by, stops to meddle with a dispute that is none of his business" (Proverbs 26:17; AMP).

A good friend of mine once asked me, "Were you invited? Did the person ask you for your opinion?" That is wisdom.

If you are not invited, the best you can do is pray about it but don't get involved.

Have you ever found yourself involved in something you were not invited into? But they need help? Well, if they do not ask for help, sometimes, all you can do is pray. Even with God, we are told to ask. Yes, the Lord may position people around others that He knows can help them, but if people do not respond or want help, unfortunately, you may have to leave them alone.

In such situations, prayer is the best one can offer a person, but getting involved with matters one is not invited to, is likely to only breed further problems. Even when invited you don't need to get involved if you feel that is the right thing to do.

"When Jesus heard it, he saith unto them, They that are whole have no need of the physician, but they that are sick: I came not to call the righteous, but sinners to repentance" (Mark 2:17).

People need to acknowledge that they need help and must want the assistance to be helped.

Chapter Eight

Forgiveness

We have no other option but to walk in forgiveness. There will always be a reason why you will have to forgive someone. The Bible reads, *And above all things have fervent love for one another, for "love will cover a multitude of sins* (1 Peter 4:8; NKJV).

There are many reasons you will have to forgive others. Sometimes, the enemy works through others, and people yield to the enemy without knowing it. We get offended sometimes because we have not grown up in certain areas.

According to Scripture, the enemy crucified Jesus Christ our Lord, but it was manifested through people (1 Corinthians 2:8). This is why Jesus Christ said, "Father forgive them, for they know not what they do" (Luke 23:34).

Despite yielding to the enemy, people are still accountable for what they do, and it's still sin. This is why Jesus Christ had to ask God to forgive them.

The same applies to us. We must forgive, walk in love, and leave things to the Lord.

Sometimes, people grow up and come back years later to ask for forgiveness. It all depends on the person's heart, whether they are tender-hearted or not. However, whether people come back and ask for forgiveness or don't is not the issue. We must walk in forgiveness at all times. The best practice is to forgive immediately. That is the best way. Unforgiveness is very dangerous and not worth its consequences (Matthew 18:24). We are to keep ourselves in the love of God at all times (Jude 21).

We are at an advantage because God's love has been shed abroad in our hearts by the Holy Spirit given unto us (Romans 5:5). And we can do all things through Christ that strengthens us (Philippians 4:13). We have what it takes.

Many years ago, 1 had to move in with some friends because 1 was travelling. One particular friend made it very clear that 1 was not wanted, and she did not hide her feelings. However, just a few years ago, she actually called to apologise. She said that she was wrong and what she did was out of order. I obviously had forgotten about it and had moved on, but 1 think 1 remembered faintly. This is just an example of what a person with a good heart and integrity will do. It shows that she has a great heart.

Who has the Lord been prompting you to pick up the phone and call, to ask them for forgiveness? Even if it happened many years ago, it does not matter. There is a reason the Lord is asking you to do something about it. Be tender-hearted and yield to what you know you ought to do.

We need wisdom in relating to people because the enemy can use people to get to us if allowed. Remember that the enemy will not come in a red hat and say "here 1 am" but will be disguised, and this can be through people.

We can see an example of this in Scripture. Remember that the enemy wanted to use Peter to divert Jesus Christ, our Lord, from His destiny. Jesus said, "Get behind me Satan". Jesus did not say "get thee behind me Peter", but "get thee behind me Satan" (Luke 4:8). Jesus nailed the attack from the root, which was through Peter.

The enemy can use people; therefore, we need discernment and wisdom when relating to others.

Chapter Nine

Honour one another

We are to honour one another and honour all men.

"Be kindly affectioned one to another with brotherly love; in honour preferring one another" (Romans 12:10).

"Honour all men. Love the brotherhood. Fear God. Honour the king" (1 Peter 2:17).

What does it mean to honour? To treat with respect. We are to relate and treat each other graciously. And if you look at the above scripture, it says, "Honour all men". All means all.

The words of our mouths are to minister life to others (Proverbs 10:21). Refuse to be the reason a person makes a lifetime decision. "So and So said this five years ago and since then, I decided...etc". This should not be us. We are children of light, and our words and the way we treat others should reflect the person of Christ.

Where we have missed it in this area, we simply need to ask for forgiveness and amend our ways.

We must also remember that we will account for every idle word we speak.

"But I say unto you, That every idle word that men shall speak, they shall give account thereof in the day of judgment" (Matthew 12:36).

"But I tell you, on the day of judgment people will have to give an accounting for every careless or useless word they speak" (Matthew 12:36; AMP).

Chapter Ten

The Power of Associations

Who we associate with matters and can affect us, whether good or bad.

Remember Solomon, the Lord warned him about taking wives from the wrong place. Unfortunately, Solomon did not listen, and it affected his heart with time.

"For it came to pass, when Solomon was old, that his wives turned away his heart after other gods: and his heart was not perfect with the Lord his God, as was the heart of David his father" (1 Kings 11:4).

His wrong associations took time to manifest, for the Bible says, "When Solomon was old".

Good relationship skills are to know when a relationship is getting dangerous and withdraw yourself from it.

"He that walketh with wise men shall be wise: but a companion of fools shall be destroyed" (Proverbs 13:20).

Walk with the wise and become wise; associate with fools and get in trouble (Proverbs 13:20; NLT).

If you want to grow in wisdom, spend time with the wise. Walk with the wicked and you'll eventually become just like them (Proverbs 13:20; TPT).

Chapter Eleven

Dealing with rejection

During His earthly ministry, Jesus Christ our Lord was rejected—"He was despised and rejected of men" (Isaiah 53:3).

"He came unto his own, and his own received him not" (John 1:11).

Being rejected of men has nothing to do with the Lord. The Lord of glory, Jesus Christ our Lord, was rejected.

Never take rejection personally; you are accepted in the beloved (Ephesians 1:6). People reject others for various reasons like lack of discernment, influence from the enemy, unwillingness to face the truth; the list goes on.

You need to stay in love. After all, you are accepted in Him. So, focus on the Lord and remain in love.

Chapter Twelve

You can't speak into everyone's life

I f you have lived and grown, you would have discovered by now that you cannot speak into everyone's life. As stated before in a previous chapter, you need permission to speak into a person's life in most cases.

What relationship do you have with them?

Did they invite you into their affairs?

In addition to that, it takes a certain type of person to receive correction. This is why we cannot speak into everyone's life. Scripture makes this clear:

"He that reproveth a scorner getteth to himself shame: and he that rebuketh a wicked man getteth himself a blot. Reprove not a scorner, lest he hate thee: rebuke a wise man, and he will love thee" (Proverbs 9:7-8).

"He who corrects and instructs a scoffer gets dishonor for himself,And he who rebukes a wicked man gets insults for himself. [ ]Do not correct a scoffer [who foolishly ridicules and takes no responsibility for his error] or he will hate you; Correct a wise man [who learns from his error], and he will love you" (Proverbs 9:7-8; AMP)

The above scripture speaks for itself. This is why we need discernment to determine whether or not we should correct a person.

Some people have corrected others and got themselves into unnecessary trouble. We really need to be wise. As mentioned before, nobody can stop you from praying for a person.

Chapter Thirteen

Dealing with misunderstandings

We live in a fallen world; we have different personalities and how we see things. Therefore, when you relate to others, there will always be a potential to be misunderstood.

We have to ensure that we always stay in love.

I heard a quote from someone many years ago, "Difference is not wrong, it's just difference".

Misunderstandings do happen. We find an account in Scripture where Paul and Barnabas had a misunderstanding.

And some days after Paul said unto Barnabas, Let us go again and visit our brethren in every city where we have preached the word of the Lord, and see how they do. And Barnabas determined to take with them John, whose surname was Mark. But Paul thought not good to take him with them, who departed from them from Pamphylia, and went not with them to the work. And the contention was so sharp between them, that they departed asunder one from the other: and so Barnabas took Mark, and sailed unto Cyprus; and Paul chose Silas, and departed, being recommended by the brethren unto the grace of God" (Acts 15:36-40).

What caused the above dispute? A difference of opinion.

There is no single way to address misunderstandings as to how it is dealt with will depend on several factors.

- Who is involved?
- The level of relationship
- Whether or not you can approach the person
- The attitude of the person

However, the golden rule of staying and walking in love applies.

Here are a few scriptures that are good templates for dealing with and handling issues.

"He that handleth a matter wisely shall find good" (Proverbs 16:20).

"Be ye therefore followers of God, as dear children; and walk in love, as Christ also hath loved us, and hath given himself for us an offering and a sacrifice to God for a sweetsmelling savour" (Ephesians 5:1-2).

"He that covereth a transgression seeketh love; But he that repeateth a matter separateth very friends" (Proverbs 17:9).

It is very dangerous to go around talking about others in a detrimental way.

"A froward man soweth strife: And a whisperer separateth chief friends" (Proverbs 16:28).

This is one thing that the Lord hates, according to Proverbs 6:19.

We are to put on love. You have to be intentional about it.

"Beyond all these things put on and wrap yourselves in [unselfish] love, which is the perfect bond of unity [for everything is bound together in agreement when each one seeks the best for others]" (Colossians 3:14).

We also need to allow others to breathe, as sometimes, people go through difficult times and act out of character because of what they are experiencing.

The following is based on a true account. However, the people involved have been given fictitious names.

Debra and her family had planned to travel abroad to see a friend of Debra. She had spoken to her friend, Joyce, and they had agreed to come over.

Debra and her family bought a non-refundable ticket to go and see Joyce and her husband. After all the arrangements, as the departure time drew closer, Debra called Joyce to make the final arrangements. But unfortunately, Joyce never picked up the phone nor returned any calls.

Debra got concerned after paying out so much and then decided to call a family member that lived in that part of the world. Graciously, the family member asked them to come and stay with him and his family.

After the holiday, Debra called Joyce, and she picked up the phone. Debra asked why she behaved like that. Her response was, "I was going through a difficult time, and I didn't want visitors". They spoke about it, and their friendship continued.

While 1 don't condone what Joyce did as she could have forewarned her friend instead of just going silent, the truth is, people go through stuff and respond differently when life happens.

We need to give people allowance, for love covers a multitude of sins.

Chapter Fourteen

Taking Heed to Warning Signs

Have you ever related to a person, and within the process of time, you notice some things which I will call "warning signs"? I am sure we have all experienced this at one time or the other.

Sometimes, things can escalate when we do not act on the initial warning signs. Therefore, we need to be sensitive to warning signs before they escalate.

A good example of this in Scripture is when Moses and Aaron approached Pharaoh to let the people of Israel go. However, as the signs began to multiply, it was obvious that Pharaoh was getting agitated.

Now, before we continue, Moses had no other option but to go back to Pharaoh because the Lord sent him, and the Lord has already forewarned him that Pharaoh will not listen (Exodus 3:19).

While we know that Pharaoh did not receive Moses' and Aaron's message, he was beginning to get agitated. If you read the account in the Book of Exodus, it got to a point where Moses and Aaron were driven from Pharaoh's presence.

"And Moses said, We will go with our young and with our old, with our sons and with our daughters, with our flocks and with our herds will we go; for we must hold a feast unto the Lord. And he said unto them, Let the Lord be so with you, as I will let you go, and your little ones: look to it; for evil is before you. Not so: go now ye that are men, and serve the Lord; for that ye did desire. And they were driven out from Pharaoh's presence" (Exodus 10:9-11).

I will call this "a warning sign" that something worst can happen. So, the Lord sent Moses and protected him and Aaron.

After this incident, when Moses and Aaron went back, the response from Pharaoh escalated.

"And Moses said, Thou must give us also sacrifices and burnt offerings, that we may sacrifice unto the Lord our God. Our cattle also shall go with us; there shall not an hoof be left behind; for thereof must we take to serve the Lord our God; and we know not with what we must serve the Lord, until we come thither. But the Lord hardened Pharaoh's heart, and he would not let them go. And Pharaoh said unto him, Get thee from me, take heed to thyself, see my face no more; for in that day thou seest my face thou shalt die. And Moses said, Thou hast spoken well, I will see thy face again no more (Exodus 10:25-29).

Looking at previous responses, Pharaoh had never driven them from his presence. After Pharaoh drove them away, the next visit had escalated to "in the day you see my face, you shall die". In the natural, if someone drove you away from their presence, the best thing to do is not to go back, but we know that Moses had to go back because he was sent, and the Lord protected him and Aaron.

Can you see how that escalated from being driven to a threat to their lives?

This is what can sometimes happen when we do not take heed to warning signs. The response from the person escalates.

You gave someone a contract to do a job for one hundred pounds, and they did not keep their word. So, why would you go ahead and give the same person a contract for one thousand pounds, then complain when the person does not deliver? It is simply because we did not take heed to the warning signs.

The following is based on a true account. However, the people involved have been given fictitious names.

Emma worked in the same office as a person called Elizabeth. In the process of time, Emma and Elizabeth became good friends. After a while, Emma got another job and told Elizabeth that she was going to resign. Elizabeth responded that she would resign too and could not work in this office without Emma being there. Emma told Elizabeth not to resign but to at least get another job before resigning, as she had a job to go on to.

Fast-forward, Emma's new job offer was confirmed, and she resigned. Elizabeth then decided to resign with no job to go unto. After Emma left, she got concerned about her friend and started looking for jobs for her friend. She will call Elizabeth and advise her on job opportunities that she was aware of that came up.

After a while, Emma noticed that the telephone conversations became dry; it was like Elizabeth did not want to talk to Emma. However, Emma persisted and thought she would leave her alone once Elizabeth got a job offer.

Then as time went on, the telephone calls started going to voicemail. Emma then got concerned about her friend as she could no longer get through to her. Then one day, Emma decided to drive down to Elizabeth's house to make sure she was okay.

Elizabeth's sister attended to her and said Elizabeth was out of the country. Emma got concerned and asked her husband, Peter, to call Elizabeth. Elizabeth picked up the phone as she thought it was an employer. Peter then said that his wife was concerned about her. Elizabeth's response was, "Tell Emma not to call my house again".

So, what can we learn from this true account?

Emma took on the responsibility of Elizabeth leaving her job which she should not have. We cannot take responsibility for other people's decisions and actions. God told Adam and Eve not to eat of the tree of the knowledge of good and evil; they alone were responsible for their own actions.

And obviously, Emma should have backed off when the telephone conversations were getting dry before they escalated to voicemail.

Many of us have been victims of not discerning warning signs. Obviously, it is not always black and white; people sometimes genuinely need help, and we cannot always take a warning sign personally. Sometimes, people are hurting and going through difficult times, which spills over into other relationships. Nevertheless, we need discernment in this area. We need to know when to back off and persist if we can help. We should also know when to refer the matter to someone that can reach the person. Above all, we need to pray.

Chapter Fifteen
Prove all things

Have you ever dived into a relationship, only to find out within time that you got yourself into a mess?

"Prove all things; hold fast that which is good" (1 Thessalonians 5:21).

"But test all things carefully [so you can recognize what is good]. Hold firmly to that which is good" (1 Thessalonians 5:21; AMP)

Most times, the reason we find ourselves in a mess is because we did not give the relationship time. We did not really know the person and just dived right in.

This scripture speaks for itself. We need to exercise discernment and judgement before committing ourselves to others. Yes, we love all men, but we do not need to commit to people hastily.

"Now when he was in Jerusalem at the passover, in the feast day, many believed in his name, when they saw the miracles which he did. But Jesus did not commit himself unto them,

because he knew all men, And needed not that any should testify of man: for he knew what was in man" (John 2:23-25).

"Because of the miraculous signs Jesus did in Jerusalem at the Passover celebration, many began to trust in him. But Jesus didn't trust them, because he knew all about people. No one needed to tell him about human nature, for he knew what was in each person's heart" (John 2:23-25; NLT).

There will always be exceptions to these principles. Sometimes, we meet people, and we just gel as they call it, and you end up getting on very well. However, proving and testing things out is wisdom before committing to others.

When Jesus Christ our Lord called His twelve disciples, while some had heard of Him before (John 1:15), others just followed Him (Luke 6:12-16). So yes, there will always be exceptions to the rule; however, just as Jesus Christ did not allow everyone to follow Him (Mark 5:19), we also need to give some relationships time to grow naturally.

Chapter Sixteen

Be Careful who you share precious things with

Has anyone ever betrayed you? You told them something in confidence, and before you realised what was happening, it became known to others?

Joseph shared his dream with the wrong people, and it cost him dearly (Genesis 37:5). It is wisdom to know who and what to share with others.

During the earthly ministry of our Lord Jesus Christ, our Lord only took three out of the twelve disciples to share special time with Him. During one of such times, these three witnessed Jesus Christ our Lord being transfigured. The Lord told them to tell "no man" until He was risen from the dead. That warning must have also extended to the other nine disciples as "no man" means "no man".

This is an example of knowing what to tell who, what, and when.

"And after six days Jesus taketh Peter, James, and John his brother, and bringeth them up into an high mountain apart,- And was transfigured before them: and his face did shine as the sun, and his raiment was white as the light. And, behold, there appeared unto them Moses and Elias talking with him.- Then answered Peter, and said unto Jesus, Lord, it is good for us to be here: if thou wilt, let us make here three tabernacles; one for thee, and one for Moses, and one for Elias. While he yet spake, behold, a bright cloud overshadowed them: and behold a voice out of the cloud, which said, This is my beloved Son, in whom I am well pleased; hear ye him. And when the disciples heard it, they fell on their face, and were sore afraid. And Jesus came and touched them, and said, Arise, and be not afraid. And when they had lifted up their eyes, they saw no man, save Jesus only. And as they came down from the mountain, Jesus charged them, saying, Tell the vision to no man, until the Son of man be risen again from the dead" (Matthew 17:1-9).

We know that God turned around what Joseph went through by telling his brothers his dreams. However, no one will argue that telling his brothers his dreams did not help Joseph.

Chapter Seventeen

Associations to avoid

The Lord has given us standards and boundaries for our own good. Did you know that the Bible warns us about certain people? Don't use the word "mercy" to expose yourself to what the Lord warns us about.

Scripture makes it clear that we need to avoid certain influences in our lives. Below are a few examples.

***

Evil communications:

"Be not deceived: evil communications corrupt good manners" (1 Corinthians 15:33).

"Do not be deceived: "Bad company corrupts good morals" (1 Corinthians 15:33; AMP).

The Lord is telling us, "Do not be deceived". In other words, do not think that it will not affect or influence you. We have no business in associating with any form of evil ways. Has the Lord been asking you to leave a certain group of people? Yes, you still love them, but you don't need to be part of them. The Lord is warning us for a reason.

***

Those that teach error:

If any man teach otherwise, and consent not to wholesome words, even the words of our Lord Jesus Christ, and to the doctrine which is according to godliness; He is proud, knowing nothing, but doting about questions and strifes of words, whereof cometh envy, strife, railings, evil surmisings, Perverse disputings of men of corrupt minds, and destitute of the truth, supposing that gain is godliness: from such withdraw thyself (1 Timothy 6:3-5).

We are told to withdraw ourselves from those that teach error.

***

Those that hold contrary doctrines to God's truth:

"Whosoever transgresseth, and abideth not in the doctrine of Christ, hath not God. He that abideth in the doctrine of Christ, he hath both the Father and the Son. If there come any unto you, and bring not this doctrine, receive him not into your house, neither bid him God speed: For he that biddeth him God speed is partaker of his evil deeds" (2 John 9-11).

There are certain people we should not be inviting into our houses.

***

Anyone called a brother practising sin:

I wrote unto you in an epistle not to company with fornicators: Yet not altogether with the fornicators of this world, or with the covetous, or extortioners, or with idolaters; for then must ye needs go out of the world. But now I have written unto you not to keep company, if any man that is called a brother be a fornicator, or covetous, or an idolator, or a railer, or a drunkard, or an extortioner; with such an one no not to eat" (1 Corinthians 5:10-13).

"When I wrote to you before, I told you not to associate with people who indulge in sexual sin. But I wasn't talking about unbelievers who indulge in sexual sin, or are greedy, or cheat people, or worship idols. You would have to leave this world to avoid people like that. I meant that you are not to associate with anyone who claims to be a believer[] yet indulges in sexual sin, or is greedy, or worships idols, or is abusive, or is

a drunkard, or cheats people. Don't even eat with such people (1 Corinthians 5:10-13; NLT).

***

Those with serious anger problems:

Don't befriend angry people   or associate with hot-tempered people, or you will learn to be like them   and endanger your soul (Proverbs 22:24-25; NLT)

Do not even associate with a man given to angry outbursts; Or go [along] with a hot-tempered man, Or you will learn his [undisciplined] ways And get yourself trapped [in a situation from which it is hard to escape (Proverbs 22: 24-25; AMP).

The above scriptures are self-explanatory. We need to be careful who we associate with.

It is evident that certain relationships need to be avoided.

But what about if they need help? Then, that is a different matter. If you are sent to minister to them or counsel them, we must obey the Lord by all means. This book addresses ongoing long-term relationships.

Chapter Eighteen

The Value of Relationships

Relationships are vital as God works through people. Our Lord Jesus Christ worked with people, and these people were called His disciples.

Have you ever heard someone say, "I just cut that person off"? While there may be genuine reasons some people are no longer in our lives, cutting a person off unnecessarily or due to immaturity can be costly. Only heaven will ascertain the people that were supposed to be in our lives that we carelessly let go of or just simply lacked discernment and did not nurture the relationship. A relationship can be a bridge that will lead you to somewhere you need to get to.

While the Lord can restore our strained relationships, provided we cooperate with the Lord, things in our lives can be delayed because of these shortfalls.

Do you remember when Paul was arrested, and the Lord told him that as Paul had testified of Jesus Christ in Jerusalem, he would do the same in Rome (Acts 23:11)? During this same period, it was Paul's Sister's son who disclosed the plot of those lying in wait for Paul to destroy him (Acts 23:16-22). See how the Lord uses people. Remember that this was not an angel but a human being the Lord used to deliver Paul. This is why we must be careful to maintain our relationships. You have no idea what the Lord wants to do through that person that the enemy or your flesh is trying to get you to be offended at.

Remember that it was Jonathan, Saul's son, who was David's best friend, that the Lord used to protect David from Saul (1 Samuel 20).

We must learn to nurture our God-given relationships and have discernment.

We are all works in progress, and to maintain most relationships, you will need the blanket of love that covers a multitude of sins (1 Peter 4:8).

Chapter Nineteen

Your gift and your tribe

We have all been given gifts (Ephesians 4:7-8; James 1:17), and these gifts are for the benefit of other people.

"As every man hath received the gift, even so minister the same one to another, as good stewards of the manifold grace of God" (1 Peter 4:10).

You will need to discern those you are called to regarding your gift. This is what is meant by the word "tribe". Those that will receive you.

Not everyone will receive you because you are not called to everyone. God has designed us uniquely (Psalm 139:14), and we need to allow the Lord to position us. We are not to impose ourselves on others.

Joseph was rightly positioned with his gift of dream interpretation, which eventually brought him to his palace (Genesis

41:1-46). However, remember that his gift of dreams caused him problems with his brothers (Genesis 37:5). While we know that Joseph was not interpreting his brothers' dreams, they could have had a better attitude when he shared his dreams with them.

Some of our relationships are quite important because they can be tied to our destinies. Therefore, we must discern and allow the Lord to position us with the relevant people for our giftings.

Making decisions based on others' reports can be dangerous

S ometimes, you need to hear a matter from both parties or all parties involved before you make a decision.

"He who answers before he hears [the facts]—It is folly and shame to him" (Proverbs 18:13; AMP).

Most people will only tell you what they want you to know, so we need to be very careful.

Except the Lord gives you insight into a matter, tread carefully before making decisions or opinions on account of one person involved.

To get the facts, you need not just one person's version of the account. Remember the love rule—"love believes the best" (1 Corinthians 13:7).

54

Chapter Twenty-one

Why is a person in your life?

I t is important to discern why a person is in your life. I know that sometimes, this can be challenging. However, we need to be careful to ensure that we maintain important relationships in our lives.

On the other hand, sometimes, people are in our lives just for what they can get. It is important to discern this to avoid what l call the "expectation gap".

"Wealth maketh many friends; but the poor is separated from his neighbour" (Proverbs 19:4).

So, why does the person in this verse have many friends? Because of their wealth. Such a person should not be disappointed if, for any reason, the wealth leaves for a season and likewise friends.

While l know that people are in our lives for more important reasons, this is just an example when suddenly, those that you thought were friends leave you.

56

Chapter Twenty-two

Conclusion

Many of us can look back and see why we have had challenges in some relationships.

While this book does not address all the issues, wisdom and discernment are crucial when relating to others.

Jesus Christ, our Lord, was rejected during His earthly ministry, but those who had discernment received Him. The greatest enemy to relationships is "lack of discernment". In other words, not discerning the value in others.

We are all valuable; don't allow anyone or any circumstance to let you think otherwise. It is simply a lie. One sacrifice was paid for all men. This shows that in the eyes of the Lord, we all hold the same value—"the cost of the blood of Jesus Christ". (Revelation 1:5).

We must honour one another and stay in love. We must walk in love because this is the evidence that we are children of God.

"We know that we have passed from death unto life, because we love the brethren. He that loveth not his brother abideth in death" (1 John 3:14).

We have what it takes because God's love has been shed abroad in our hearts by the Holy Spirit given unto us (Romans 5:5).

We are children of God, and God is love!

Salvation Prayer

F ather God, I come to you in Jesus' name. I admit that I am a sinner, and I now receive the sacrifice that Jesus Christ paid for me.

I confess with my mouth the Lord Jesus, and I believe in my heart that God raised Him from the dead.

I now declare that Jesus Christ is my Lord and Saviour.

Thank you, Father, for saving me in Jesus' name.

I am now your child. Amen.

bisiwriter@outlook.com. Start reading your Bible and ask the Lord to guide you to a good church.

About The Author

Bisi Oladipupo has been a Christian for many years and lives in the United Kingdom with her family.

Bisi attended a few Bible colleges, and she has completed a diploma in Biblical Studies from a UK Bible college.

She is a teacher of God's Word, coordinates Bible studies, and has a YouTube channel at https://www.youtube.com/c/BisiOladipupo123.

She writes regularly, and her website is www.inspired-words.org

Her author page is www.bisiwriter.com

You can contact Bisi by email at bisiwriter@outlook.com.

Other Books by Bisi

The Twelve Apostles of Jesus Christ: Lessons We Can Learn

The Lord's Cup in Communion: The Significance of taking the Lord's Supper

Different Ways To Receive Healing From Scripture and Walk in Health

Believing on The Name of Jesus Christ: What Every Believer Needs
to Know

The Mind and your Christian Walk: The Impact of the mind on our
Christian walk